On The Edge Of A Dream

by Atalie Rachael

On The Edge of a Dream - Atalie Rachael

Introduction

— ✿ ❀ —

We are all a passionate piece of poetry waiting to be written. We constantly lie in wait for a rhythm, so that it may guide us from youth to death. We hunt for ourselves by the hour, trying to figure out the stitches and patterns that make us unique. We stumble sometimes on our noses, because the answer is right in front, and yet we keep polishing the rear-view.

We fight, we feel, and sometimes we grind ourselves into an impalpable mess.

That is what poetry does. It is an outlet for all of these things. It is the existential matter of life that provides people and poetry with true meaning. At times, it is the lifeline that some of us can never quite let go of.

To The Reader

—  —

The main themes contained in this book resolve to explain growing, learning, and making positives out of pain. Some of it is bitter, and some of it is sweet. Few parts are reflective, and others more on the romantic side. This book is a flawed belief in versatility, but nevertheless a permanent one. This book is naive, but uniquely experienced. These pages are acceptance of life, nature, and the human element. And the words within are five long deserted years, editing the screeches of personal growth and observational mindfulness. Abstracts sometimes remove the constricts of emptiness. But with that removal came a dream more powerful than anything else: a well worded flight into freedom.

This is the edge of a dream.

Dedicated to my parents
and my best friend Alyssa

— ❦ *Part 1* ❦ —

The Dream, The Struggle, The Ache   9

— ❦ *Interlude* ❦ —

Dream Of Incarcerated Things   114

— ❦ *Part 2* ❦ —

The Lesson, The Becoming, The Truth   117

On The Edge Of A Dream

Not A Morning Person

The morning mimics me as I awaken.

I see it before me:

    Left hand on its hip,

            right hand brushing its teeth,

looking oddly off into the distance,

pretending to be writing poetry

in the same exact way I would.

    6:49 AM.

I roll over and suddenly it's as if

someone is beating my brains to a

pulp to keep me from dreaming.

The twit won't stop singing

and thrusting open the curtains.

She lets all of the dawn and its

members into my room.

There is now a restless chatter

about how

    the trees have ironed their leaves,

        and

the rosebuds have opened out to the sun,

stretching to feel its playful bite of a kiss

It's all too much.

If mornings are always going to

be this intrusive and happy,

then why am I so bitter over here?

My breath even smells like

a dying dog.

Springtime Speech

Spring sometimes is a loveless nest,

with but a few twigs of some

shocked arteries.

To the full it is positive and with hope

that new life will cast this aging planet,

by nature things will grow,

and everything will find its

green and its blossom.

But how damned well does one

get by the first tones

in the speech

of springtime?

That loneliness is living and rising,

and living and rising

again.

Finding Myself In Detroit

Grizzly vines clamoured

upon the house front.

Graffiti slandered against the brick.

Bankruptcy is picturesque

against a sidewalk of burnt-out cigarettes.

Corners. Streets. Pillows.

Here lies the lonely ghetto.

I just wish I could

crawl out of my white skin

so they wouldn't stare

at me so.

Becoming Sunshine

"Have you talked to her?"

Yes, I've talked to her.

The sun.

It was just yesterday,

as I was walking through the thrush,

that she told me she gets cloudy sometimes.

And she asked me to take her place

if such an occurrence

should happen.

Passing Asylum

Often times, the grandeur of my breath
holds a billion unsought words.
Those that make the seeing more vivid,
the hearing more pronounced.
But to speak,
I'm an infant without knowledge
and I somehow believe these words will never pour forth.

But what does pour today
is the rain.
It makes noises upon the chimney
like one who rearranges the silverware drawer.
Seemingly, it speaks for me,
letting me hold my breath and lay
back unto its drifting pelt upon the roof.

The shy bird nearest my window
has just been born, and its life is three weeks.
He has a crisp way about his shuffling this morning.
Purpose.
His chirp is not hungry, but it is sweet.
I think he's going to rise from the nest

and get wet.
For between each raindrop is desideratum.

His running will turn to flying,
and his flying will turn to democracy.

Oh,
you darling whitetail,

wait for me!

Take F(light)

If faith is not the embassy of liberty,

then how will anything ever be

alright?

I have learned that you must believe

before doing that which you may

desire least.

Does not the robin do so before

she nestles her eggs?

And does not the pear withhold

its cowardliness before landing

upon the earth's floor?

Heed ye, the arrival of others before you,

and notice complexion.

Its flush created our world,

in all the savory blushed color forms

that the songbird sings to

when freedom writhes under

the morning skin.

The Sun Kissed Me Today

Sights and sounds

dreaming up something worthwhile.

Hello, you human over yonder!

Life!

There's so much *life* in life.

A vibrant vision, startling even eternity.

The temptation

to be alive

burns through the aggravation.

There's a *life* in love.

There's a *love* in life.

Your time is a wild but short one,

embracing juncture's ravish.

Simple things make a wholesome dwelling,

but at times, gratitude

is the greatest thing

that can see you through.

wild

Being normal is f u t i l e,

when in each and every one

of us lies a wonderous

streak of m i s a d v e n t u r e.

When You Meet A New Friend

Opaque is a color pulled up

from the grassroots of neighborhoods

we build inside.

Greeting one another with our

gardening gloves still sewn to our wrists,

we try to figure through

the beauty that stings us all

at least once.

A Spool Of Awe

I met a beauty so wild today.

So full of ease,

adventure,

that my language had ceased

shy belonging.

Still water,

so sparkling with mischief

that a haiku

wouldn't budge its flow.

A proverb couldn't prove its sin,

for none was there

in this breathless dance.

Slow dance a-moving, the wild was.

That meaning dropped,

flew,

caught itself on a spool of awe

and forgot—altogether

completely

—the feeling it gracefully laid upon me.

My yearning

was prodded and shaped

into something like joyful weakness.

For I was joyful,

but submitting.

The wild wanted to talk with me

a minute.

For apparently, a simple goose would not suffice.

A Happy Euphemism

The kitchen suddenly

became quiet

as the flowers peeped

through the windows,

asking to be let in

and placed upon the

dinner table.

Kill It Or Cure It

You look sweet.

You look innocent.

Though my eyes may lie,

the thought hither went.

For the night, the dusk,

you could mend me

'til I am satisfied

of chasing you regretfully.

Spiritual Journey

I placed the stethoscope

upon my soul

and hesitated, wondering

if it really was okay

to do so.

Take a few glances around,

just to make sure

that they know not of

anything they heard.

Chimera's Demise

A myth is the embodiment of nature

before it was a form of proof.

For in the moment one disproves a myth,

they destroy a beautiful calm

only to find truth,

a light unsought between the ceilings

of the world.

Looking And Speaking

Such the tangled mess that I am;

I forget my words when

basking in your presence.

Picking at scabs of scars,

I feel like the absent minded crow,

frowning at life for naught

while you sit beside looking like

a breathtaking picture

of all the character qualities

I'd easily become smitten with.

If it weren't suddenly that something

placed bricks against my lips,

and kept them from

opening and speaking

all the things I adore about you.

Oh, but I am looking.

and I am speaking.

It's just that my eyes are

doing it better than the

rest of me dares to.

A Moment Of Silence

"How do you feel?"

You're asking me.

. . .

Truth is, my love,

one cannot simply arrange

feelings like compartmentalized

little specks waiting to be

sniffed out by those so willing

to answer their own

question.

It's an earthquake in here

and you cannot sugarcoat

tall ceilings and pillared shambles

when it all tends to lay in a heap.

How do I feel?

Well, I can't make sense out of

what I don't understand.

For now, it will be enough

if we have a moment of silence.

Don't hold your breath.

Just breathe with me.

Smoking in the Evening

The windows of the wind

are open.

As I look through,

I see the moon breaking

its heart

for me to fall in love

with it.

When Love Takes Its Time

When love takes its time,

it is a polite thing at first.

And it grows.

But not like a seed.

Not like a tree,

a blossom, a caterpillar,

etc.

Those are all things that

metaphors have

started to yawn upon.

No, let us put it this way.

Love is a reaping in which

sometimes you don't sow.

You reap and you reap.

Politeness, adoration,

war, growth.

It all but collides together like a crash course

filled mess; you reap,

not what you sow,

but you reap destiny.

Day by blessed day.

Night by cursed night.

Your shoulder blades may groan

under the brunt of such

a progressive love.

The blinds of your soul may

get dusty,

age, yellow,

and yet destiny is not an end.

It is infinity.

This kismet may start as politeness

and continue as a bowl of soup

you both share in the evening

reveling in all the years stolen together.

Simple Peace

I can hear our breaths

being interchanged,

like little small gifts

unwrapping themselves unto

the emptiness of the

silence, quietly hanging.

Almost like wall decor

without any fancy splendor.

Just pure simple peace,

outlined in an anxious world

of hurry, bustle, go.

But they indeed do not

understand that no movement

is needed in a room,

when two beings can just

sit within and enjoy each

other's company.

Eternity

I felt that I had died

But I never did.

The sweetest love revived

Would surely never quit.

Fighting Forces

When my stalking heart learned of loyalty,

it sank within its depths;

its forests of fighting

and confused choking breaths.

For this new task seemed hard in conquering.

I cannot be free

to give the very heart

that another gave to me.

Brethren

Brethren are men

that hold the world

in its throat

with one hand,

and with the other,

their woman;

so lovingly close

that she can smell

his aftershave.

This Moment

Paper fingers and wooden legs

dance slow in a riding car,

like an only definition of my

young confused mind.

Taking in the sights and sounds,

like a new piece of property

destined for childish footsteps.

Crackling fires underneath

s'mores and laughter.

And to think of these things

while the sunshine dances in

a dream upon my tiny notepad;

it is only small enough for me

to close my eyes in traffic

and smile.

Road Runner

Roads are mysterious

little prayers we say to ourselves

to stay at home in hopes of

never actually

getting lost.

The Map

It's riveting the way

    the map seems to itch for our lingering eyes

        to follow its destination.

There is no haste in the way

    it curves and turns.

        And yet so quick it will

hold us by the hands of our

    imagination.

        By our heartstrings so docile,

the half-coffee-stained, half-pointed

    shape of the needle still southern

        in its willful prompt down

            memory lane.

Innocently, this mere paper

    crumpled from a few numbered grabs

        to seek with a squinted desperation.

It's meaning decoded to

    simple directions of hope

and shame.

It's riveting how so carefully

    and so carelessly our senses tingle

        as if feathered by danger

and electrified by the first kiss

    of destiny.

        Indeed, the map has a way

of choosing us for letting go.

    In a moment of fatality,

        mortality has lost the high ground too, and

faith becomes a compass

    leading the way to

        eternity.

Winning Smile

My soul is like that of a wide field

who wanders on and on as if lost at sea,

finding harbor only at the end of the sunset.

Heels softly feeling all the abundant grass below;

I run as if I could actually finally grab

a ray of sunshine, take it home with me,

lay it on my floor, put it in my vase, and

watch it flower like a dandelion herb blossoming

into courage. The strength to run my heart back

across the padded green again tomorrow and

find what there is to see—feel what there is to

feel. Grab the light another way and make it brighter,

radiate it out while praying you'll catch it, you'll

make use of it, and you'll be uplifted by it. Maybe

we can race each other and see who wins

at smiling bigger from the soul

inside and out.

Harmony

The honeybee is a choir

in all its growing, tasting,

and pollinating.

Acquiring the flower beneath,

he knows how to

settle the sting in his teeth

and sweeten the tribe

carried in his intentions

to the wildflower underneath.

Hand It Over

There is such a joy in saying

    "Hand it over,"

        and his palm touches yours

            and the knuckles interlace.

Autunno

Drifting across,

feeling the bottom under my feet,

the surface

of the wooden planks.

Proof unbeknownst to me

that seasons do change,

because it creaks more

as it swells.

Down hallways,

shy steps to the bedroom,

laying down

for a nap against you;

the warmth in our beings

settled into the pew.

Your heartbeat

sounds like the soft back and forth

swish-sweesh

of someone sweeping the floor.

It's here.

On The Edge of a Dream - Atalie Rachael

A syndrome of autumn.

Curled up comfortably

against an ulterior symptom.

And still,

the creaking and the sweeping,

it's reminiscent

of being gifted with

a little bit of heaven.

Perpetual Beauty

I am an expert

in tracing the veins

of your hands to the

stemmed nerves of

your heart.

Here in this quite

moment, I find

the stillness of the

company we make

an unaltered art.

Six Senses

Sometimes I am my lungs,

when the sweet atmosphere around me closes in.

Evergreens. Rain. Roses.

I can smell my man's sweatshirt

from at least a thousand miles.

Sometimes I am my touch,

when nature's protrusions yearn at me so.

Paper leaves. Skin. Flows.

I can graze it all so fleetingly

and feel the outcome for an eternity.

Sometimes I am my tastebuds,

when the table holds a delicate meal.

Strawberries. Lips. Tea bubbling.

Each morsel is a moral

I can slowly lick my chops around.

Sometimes I am my ears,

when instinct whispers softly around corners.

Fire. Cracklings. Newspaper ash.

I can tune out the dialect of a storm,

except for his wry voice mumbling exceptional things.

Sometimes I am my eyes,

when the dusk casts away nocturnal tides.

Savory. Birds. Sunsets.

I can steal the hints of all that I see

and paint it anew.

And lastly,

sometimes I am my heart;

slumbering amongst my feelings.

Startled. Petrified. Longing.

I can cry it sober or laugh it joyful.

This sixth sense...

O, tis' such a handful!

Young Bodies

Spider in the roses

(young bodies with old souls

always notice).

The little wild things

that creep

like the mosquito

when it sings.

The mild mammal without sleep

chewing the morning,

taken by

tender thoughts too deep.

The natural world with

beautiful brokenness

and

young bodies with old souls

always notice.

It's A Time To Pick Apples

Hummingbirds atop the tree limbs

with feverish descent.

    Slowly, the picker observes its own.

Mornings are prime

for telegrams to be sent.

One particular apple tastes

like words on the way.

    Be them special or negligent,

naught they should waste

time's earnest decay.

The town has a fire

way deep down in its stomach.

    Eager to eavesdrop

a predator silent,

but the prey is surely specific.

Picking season once was

a pure spectacle of living.

    Catch your earn, earn your keep;

today it's a war reform.

Even if it's just apple picking.

Wine Tasting

Bitter with a drop of vinaigrette,

though at the back of the tongue

remains a sweetness like grace.

Like leaf and in between a charm

of splashed raspberry, mixed

finally with a saucy tea;

herbal cinnamon red parfait.

Darling,

you're flawed,

but I drink to you.

Open Scars

Somewhere in the cracked moss

under your feet,

lies within lies

Whatever do you see?

If it weren't that sorrow burns

like the wind,

or the colors of rain hitting

your skin,

wouldn't you say

it's unfortunate how my words run

deeper than you think?

Fleshly Wont

The days are kindred spirits,

the nights an unpressed brew.

Back to back, spines clicked.

Things that our teachers knew.

Within the days contain mortality.

And mortality, she is advice in flesh;

wanting—and constantly is sin

that which picks at bones in a rush.

Advice is a thwarted high note,

her melody rich with poisons seduce.

A mindful one is to beware:

Pride has its own shade of rogue.

Uncomfortable

There lies an unspoken void

waiting for something deep,

something true.

The cavities of the heart

ask for slow music,

something new.

A thing to be tapped into,

drunk from,

and fulfilled by.

A certain extent featured,

awakened

and renewed by.

But it only prowls a season

before something twinkles

in attention.

Catching the matter in spanned,

the mind finds

a new affection.

Affected by distraction,

an inside being

lacks quiet tastes.

Runs, surely it flees

to ample interests

and silly wastes.

Now, the soul is

back to where

it started.

Ill-contented in all things

and generally disheartened.

The Needs Of A Woman

Grace, fancy, and splendor

across her rising and falling chest.

You've failed to tell her

what she actually means to you.

You'll find her humble

romanticism

only willing to go so far

before she realizes

you've taken her for granted,

yet again.

The Drowning

Pieces of emotion

and scraps of poetry

sit at the dwindled bottom

of the silver pot.

It is started with firstly

a short long lived simmer,

increasing to a boil

'til finally spilling over the sides

in a mass as big as two tusks.

Finally, the waves are

rocking gently in my mouth.

Every so now and again they lap at

the shores of my lips,

reminding me there is a picture of

you that is an almost entrance

to the harbor of our beginning.

You were everything and mine and more.

But friend, you are so much older

and yet your knowledge of life resembles

your baby front tooth;

tiny and inconceivable of

the shark that prods between my waters.

I cannot explain how the emblem of my

being is like a boat centered with splitting

sides, and oddly enough you sure rocked

me as good as hell.

I just wish my instinct would row

me out.

Nervous

Magenta tips

tracing the list

of unreturned phone calls.

The snow is

chasing my headlights

down shallow streets,

and the leftovers

of yesterday's picnic

are spoils of conversations

you refused to have.

You laughed

when I suggested

that loyalty be

the centerpiece

of our love.

The nerve

of your laughter!

The same nerve

that made sure

I could never trust again;

and instead forewarn

every other man

that my curves come

with a price.

I dare him

on a simple whim

to *just be true.*

For who is she

that I am less than?

When I am the vow

that would keep love

to keep loving you

again and again.

The Murder

You're a murder,

the way you look at me.

All the rattled words you cannot find

slithering between knit gaps in your teeth.

I wonder how you speak of me

In the presence of an unholy well

that we call a world?

For a wellspring knows its place.

To give refreshment,

but to also get a little murky.

Darling,

You're a timelapse

crashing into my aching arms.

Here—but gone.

The way you pull away, it's liable

to cause a gal harm.

But back to my original point:

How do you speak of me?

With love, or with speechless frays

catching on doorknobs?

Hate To Love (YOU)

Tonight you will sleep

in the scream that sits

in my throat;

silently howling with

the pressure of your

name, wanting to take off

from my tongue like some

jet ski aloft

and free.

The Lonely Lonely

It's a cold rain.

It's a casting spell.

It's a deep ache.

It's a bottomless hell.

The lonely lonely

are only those,

they that can tell.

It's a falling waste.

It's a dying melt.

It's a hardened day.

It's a drying well.

The lonely lonely

are only those,

they that can tell.

Surrender

I'm

    going

        to

            leave

                love

                    to

                        itself.

Between Throes

You cannot create pain.

Pain will create you.

If pain has not created you,

then you will create pain.

If such inflicted pain that you create

has not hurt you,

then you will never feel pain.

If pain has hurt you,

it therefore has created you.

And it may come in years.

And it may present itself in decades.

Pain does not lie

unless it lies within you.

It is true of course that you

may cause your own pain.

But in the end pain will create you.

If you are a partaker, a trader,

and betrayer of pain, then so what has

it done to you for you to do to it

what it has done to someone else?

If you create pain

you are incapable of feeling pain.

But if you cannot create pain

then pain will create you.

Tendency

Everything sits inside me,

collecting bad habits.

It teaches one

to not leave alone

those that are lonely.

That, has yet to make its

way past my stubborn knots.

Only this.

What forbidden cast of pride

must it take to admit

how barren everything swallows

to the fetal position

of our insides?

For everything I am

has but rot, not grown.

It stands complacent,

per usual,

collecting bad habits.

The Plague of Influence

Chasing at the emerald water

'til it hisses at your fingertips.

A pretty matter is a snake

planting poison upon your lips.

What is influence without you

to give into its twilight stare?

To feed its embodied roots,

so that it sprouts bereft of air?

Spilling Denial and all Its Nettles

Illusions of dark strays

and scented earths,

with no sight beyond a paper bay

and unwalked turfs.

Heaven came down for a minute

to dine with us.

She said she loved our love.

And she stole our trust.

My sneakers are still over there,

beside your Converse.

Untouched since we last ran the stairs

down to the kitchen verse.

Reading it like a hymn song

and taking out tonight's dinner.

The exploit goes daylong

and nighttime is the new winter.

Heaven did it, honey.

Never our nerve to take this route.

Did we not study?

Breathe it all—sin, sweet like aged fruit.

Not I, neither you dearie.

We merely chanced the world together;

gave it all in nature's way.

Surely, you'd remember?

Radio Sadness

The radio makes me sad

at night.

Though I warn the lonesome

away,

no lullaby will do

to wave goodbye to you.

The radio makes me sad

at night,

when chasing stations is like

chasing Saturn—

futility is a fool

and not a lullaby will do.

For the radio sadness

is an inconspicuous tool

to get me blue for you.

Not a jagged tune

can pull me through.

A jazz pick-me-up

is a bad pull-me-down;

a soulful melody

is a haunted sound.

The radio makes me sad

at night

and the sadness is you.

Parts Of Pieces

Saturated by the appeal of longing,

I've sat down upon the steps;

they that send tingles of memories.

And indeed, I've longed.

Longed for a sweet, a one sweet

morning; waking up not with a

silly dry lump in my throat of loneliness,

but of a feeling of resting.

Beside a soul that I were for once

allowed to cherish as my own.

I could get the coffee brewing

and froth into it his favorite creamer.

If he prefers it black,

the morning dew will be enough

to carry our seeking frames outdoors;

sit a bit, hand hold a bit, and breathe.

But how far can longing go?

This, I ask myself.

For if I were never happy alone,

then I'll never be happy with him.

I've suddenly begun to realize

that I may be broke.

Just as if a watch needed mending,

the parts of pieces of me do, too.

Because sadly,

You have to get along with yourself

before you can get along with anyone else.

Attention Seeker

You over pout your lips

with your chestnut crayon

and glaze your eyelids

with shimmery sands.

But who are you really hiding from?

Who are you *really*,

if you so constantly

disguise your freckled flaws

and grasp for the approval

of no one who cares?

Chameleon

Something smells sweet,

    but

        you

            look

                like

                    a lie.

Ladies In A Room

I have seen the ladies in a room

gathered together

like bridgework settled against one's

teeth.

Prim and proper,

dainty and neat.

Fanning themselves with mortality

as the discussion turns its tide

in the dozen little sips of coffee

between pausings.

And often one has to wonder at

their place here.

How out of touch the setting seems.

Fluent and righteous—

self righteous, that is.

Simply shooting the breeze

becomes toxic waste.

If there underlies in this room

a hypocrite,

such a lady heed no right

to present herself as moral

if she speaks with a two-colored

tongue.

But naturally, the afternoon gossip

will only continue.

With just maybe a bit more sugar

for the coffee though.

Sweet Spot

Shake down.

Shake down my wild longing

from that there tree.

Too long it has

proclaimed a fool out of me.

Cursed spine.

Cursed spine that sups maturity

given sprout as a root.

O' to loathe

mineself now, and to miss the

sweet days.

With the sweet spots

(innocent and without womanliness);

to that I say:

"Blast being a woman!"

Roots of Struggle

They all talk of how to stay younger

and I rather tire of it.

We are victims to an idolized ill-reality

that will not allow us to comfortably sit.

I'd rather grow with the lions

somewhere in a deep west muse.

Toughen me as if I were twine—

made for stronger, so as to

not confuse.

This profound roar at the moon is proof

that youth has no place in a jungle.

The trees have silhouettes that agree,

and age is mortality settled into a

root of struggle.

I am amused.

Youth?

Depart from me.

On The Edge of a Dream - Atalie Rachael

My soul lies weary.

The Problem

The problem with

you and me

is that I'm not you

and you're not me.

Lasciviousness

A man's mind is a behemoth malignant

caught in the red dark of flares and

snares.

It only expands when desiring—at moments

—whatever it prides itself on; whatever catches

it unaware.

Be it a simple dress pertained tightly,

to the wave of a hand; the heat has

no hesitation.

It's planned and it's schemed seven times

before the blink of an eye, then spite

proceeds with invitation.

Because she turned away, paid you no further

attention, and said no.

And a man does what any man does:

Continues in thought as he turns

to go.

Astringency

I scathed your insides

like a delicate thorn.

Petting your delicious words

in pretty form.

But naive souls tend to

revengefully turn

when you, who with advantage,

prey upon discern.

The matter detailed at

forthwith,

and yet still your own

conscience you forfeit.

With sneering jabs,

veneered by laughs;

I no longer find you

funny, friend.

The Woman Makes The Woman

What is it you're trying to say?

That estrogen is but a prime thing?

For what else can it create,

besides curves and children?

It's not what one can say,

but rather the actions they bring

to the table.

Her table,

built around her ribs.

All graced with invitation understand

it is futile

to dress her and toss her

onto the center,

jewel her and laden her

with all the decorations.

And the nerve it must take

to settle her before all in poise.

The disdain

you must have to create this

when you know full well

in it lies no difference.

When it's the woman

that makes the woman.

Not you.

To Those In Judgment

Unfavorable politics

by scheming minds.

I find them distasteful,

Ma'dam.

But you didn't really

know that, did you?

Pride and disrespect

from those opinionated

enough to object,

they make me heave

terribly, Sir.

But you either know

not of this.

You only know that I

appear young,

feminine, and of course

much too silly to care

about these matters.

Oh how

the world is such an

unfair place!

Inferno Rise

Cackling mindless little fires.

Each and every one spitting

like singed hatred.

        That's what you do.

        That's what you are.

When the only reverb in the

room is a silent burning—

all of the ashes slowly

falling away, like levels

of flights crash—hiss

to the bare ground.

        This is what you do.

        This is what you are.

A depthless space filling

my curvy contours

with the nerve to tell

me that I should change.

This is what I do.

This is what I am.

Do not expect emulation

and imitation; for my sides

of me——my stairs——they

no longer forsake me,

because I keep climbing

even as I burn.

The Coward

A skeleton.

You lost your dignity

with your flesh.

You are mere bones

Jutting out

your own spectacle of a

Self.

Running, leaving behind

a sight.

The others appreciate

this advantage

to their own

Humor.

You shalt ever inherit

much worth,

lest you at least

grow a thick skin.

Night Air

The blessed night air

seems to stick to the

molecules in my lungs.

Begging and asking,

instinct tells when to

breathe   deeper.

When to   let go.

When to   cease

the fight against life.

Wondrous night air

breaks one free.

A monumental minute

without   care.

Without   worry.

Hesitation is merely

a wrong road turn

amidst the sky of

stars blinking warmly.

Almost like inviting a

stranger—whether he

be broke, she be heartless.

Whether both need

simply a warm drink.

All tells patiently,

a pleading to just

rest a little.

Just   a little...

Resting is a Blessing

It seems almost impossible to move,

for I might disturb the peace of my

sleepy revel in depression.

Even if I opened one eye, the movement

feels as sour as an unraptured church.

All of my bones solemnly bow and hum

in a rather destitute but determined

way. But the hypocrite of a soul I

have stirs as if it may rise,

and yet it never does.

What a beloved liar.

I should probably make some coffee

now, and have a few bites to nourish

myself. But instead, I'm brewing my

own pot of self pity and nibbling at

the salty frost of a few tears.

I could rationalize that I'm laying

here resting, and that resting is a

blessing—that is, if you happen to

ignore the turmoils of life
and exist within your own spiritual creation.
But it's false if one sits in a garden
and sees the bounty of colorful
sustenance around them. The elderberries,
for example. They glisten in the late
year as if to promise a positive reckoning.
You can taste them, and feel them
mapping their way down your gullet,
but you cannot grab them when you're
in your own straitjacket.
But resting is a blessing, even if it means
slipping into a world beneath yourself
in order to divide the pain by half.
Resting is indeed a blessing.

Let Thy Heart Bleed

When you chastise yourself

for not being strong enough,

sometimes it helps to remember

that sadness is more human

than strength.

News Weak

Love is a headline,

but I'm not going to read

the news today.

Instead, I'm going to listen

to the crisp reminder

telling me I need a break.

It may not crinkle as invitingly

as a newspaper would

when you go to open it,

but it sifts itself like

soft grain behind my tender neck;

sounding a little bit

like stolen breezes from the

quiet and trembling night.

It's not much,

but it's noncommittal,

and that alone finds my loyalty.

Hate is a headline,

On The Edge of a Dream - Atalie Rachael

but I'm not reading anymore.

At this point I'm caught in the

throes of unreliability,

and in keeping have found

the stale echoes

a little

like a sudoku puzzle:

Mundane and poised.

All these pages turning,

sifting, and swiping.

Without nibbling at the thought,

a break sounds like my own dream

cascading across the front gazette

in fine quill-stained scrawl.

But,

I am not going to read the news.

Not today.

To be Alone When You're Alone

My cheeks burn

at all of the thoughts I never asked to have.

A heartless demeanor gets one into trouble

when it takes a particular moment to warm up

your insides,

better than any stiff drink ever could.

Suddenly,

the blood is flowing swifter than any red sea.

Longing is a local shore

to swim to.

It's all too much right now.

Too much.

If the sand aside

would only welcome me a minute,

I'd build my castle there

and cure my tummy

of all its ulcers that refused new life-bound love.

What I mean is;

to be alone when you are alone,

you kind of have to be alone even more to carry on.

Right now my back hurts

because located in front of it is my heart,

and I need to work on my posture.

A Story of Skin

I shelter you with the color

that you are.

I protect you from disease

that causeth harm.

I surround your body in

every single inch.

Soft to callous, flawed rough,

feeling every pinch.

Physically to spiritually, I

bore you confident

amongst hideous stares; the

insult assault provident.

I heard all they pointed at,

said, and beat.

I didn't betray you, we were

the same meat.

Together sheltered and unsheltered,

we felt spit.

On the ground, choked to the wall.

Punches, continued hits.

They battered us because color,

it was you.

Beneath me, it was the person

of very few.

I protect us because of who and

what we are.

And I'd do it again, because

I am your skin.

And I'd do it again and again,

because I shelter what's

from within.

Iota

Every grass blade

is about learning to grow

once we've been

cut.

Let Mine Self Adrift

My head is filled with softly draining kettle pots,

humming as they empty into the washbasins;

quietly prodding between the nerves of hair

that sit on top.

My head no longer wants war,

for it is a tired thing.

But indeed I can almost hear

the echos inside, purring

like some distilling process

telling all through the rest

of the hallways and rooms

to bid a temporary farewell.

Sleep against the waves,

and tumultuous as they may be,

they are drained of today's inadequacies.

Vineyard Vacancy

I'm vacant within my

turmoil,

finding heart-stained nouns

in bleeding soil.

The fervor with which

feelings run, express,

and explain.

It burns like a black

hole, fiery depth,

sweet pain.

Darling,

this vineyard has seen its time.

Why don't we sell it

along with the years

we toiled

together?

Heart Sober

My, my!

I've lain about

the things I've figured out.

Being heart sober

may render me senseless.

Interlude

— ✿ ❁ —

Dream of incarcerated things. Not the things that require the taking of life itself, but the things that bring all the weatherly wild out of your imagination.

Pretend that there is something about green tea. Imagine your internal wanderings, where they would lead you. See the world outside of what everyone told you to see it for. Including what you're reading right now. These are merely words with reason.

Actively, I perceive nothing in the interests that I'm telling you what to do, but rather that something external guides you along the ridges of what lies indoors. Your home holds a mind with unread book spines and upholstered dust.

Life is full of vines. Each genius species spiraling into petals, putting a beautiful choke on your every dream, thought, or awakening. And, oh! Do you ever let those beautiful vines take over. Some of them you have a great rapport with. So much so, that they indefinitely rape your own will to become the artist within you.

To dream of an incarcerated thing is to bring out the gush of life and hold it sensibly between palm and heart. Be that the morning meditation wherein the chirrup of the blue jay preys on your senses and gives peace to oxygen. Or be it the canvas. The actor. The engineering of architecture. These things do not flit about, for they within themselves wouldn't find it easy to do so.

It is the incarcerated thing that must be dug from the soil, as the worm from its mineral home. It is only after that has been accomplished does the outcome look easy. Dream of incarcerated things, my friend. I plead with you! Find them, bring them out, and release the shackles. Your dream must have a haircut, new clothes, and some berries from the garden. It must learn new waltzes. It must stand for freedom. It must sing to all the world. Be the lyrics. The storm. The desire. All of these ideals do not demand ease, but instead a day at a time to get to the end of the idea itself. Continue to feel as if you've yet to create the greatest thing. There will always be orchards, and growth, and spirits

rooted in all our inner children within us. Teach incarceration to prance in endless fields, and it will keep finding new footprints within the world of hum and sunflowers.

—  —

Slipping Out Of The Coma

Starting to take pride in being alone

with my thoughts.

Starting to find openings in the salt

of my pores.

Giving criticism a pass, and expectation

a final wave.

Leaning out by direction, stepping another

city beneath me.

Staggering in a well built illusion,

but awake inside.

Starting to meditate upon the chapters

of imperfection.

Learning patience is a place

of discipled mistakes.

Starting to feel the earth once more.

It rotates in my soul.

Saving Spaces

I'm not going to lie.

My skin is starting to feel like a

sweater as I feel along its

fabric.

Flawed, rough, smooth;

the follicles of the micro stitching.

Bumps and scars accompany pin

pricks.

It is becoming safe.

Safer to inhibit the warmth layered

atop my reckless criss-crossed

veins.

Invited, sampled, felt.

You can touch it too, but to wear?

I'd rather honor the space, the island,

the only shelter around my

rolling plains.

The Storm Never Hides

Have you ever noticed how when

a storm begins to rustle around the

edges of the hemisphere, she never hides?

She starts slowly. She gathers her clouds

and reasserts them as if they were the

folds, the tucks, the fabric of a gown;

wedding white, all neatly draped

around her blue shoulders.

Next, she ruffles the tops of the trees; surely she does,

but she starts slow as if

to feel her very soul evade by her fingertips

through and through, to breathe her breath.

The leaves now have this distinct life.

Alive, almost untethered and forthcoming

to greet the existence of magnificence.

Now she'll cast the wind about her neck,

like an invisible pearl swirling and resting;

bouts between a dream

and a reality.

Her wind grazes everyone, from the merest kiss to the skin, to the flyaway hat that now sent the sailor cursing over his woebegone loss instead of catching his hoarded oxygen to at least notice that her wind is a thing of wonder. So, on and all it went, and now the cities of Earth start to tremble. Flickering lights and shaky houses all realize they got to play with her hair at some point. The rolling thunder begs escape from her graceful lips; the embers of electricity flow from her queenish heart like a poker game. She has no reason to seek shelter when she is the shelter and the war all at once.

Red Bird

I was startled by a red bird.

Be-settled himself he was,

against a sea of leaves.

I noticed how a feast

he was for the eyes.

Especially for those pertained

to closing, for a dire day

creates a broken spirit.

And mine—sought as it was

by need—couldn't help chasing

the dainty red bird up to the sky,

where he rode with an aeroplane

to get his morning dose

of the sun.

Carelessness

Idle palms stay mushy.

Lazy hands stay still.

But careless hands turn

ugly when they are

not used to save a

life.

Don't You Know? We Write

When we are a content people,

the crevices of our words

take on different shapes.

They sprawl and they jump.

Sometimes providing relief,

sometimes taking from our throats

and forming a sort of lump.

One that is swallowed and

digested into courage

to tell a story.

To tell our story.

Subaqueous

At this very hour,

I have life between my fingertips

in all its bittersweet bliss.

At this moment,

I have nothing to strive for

but the ache of paper.

Even at this very second,

I am a poetic vase

filled to the empty face.

Waiting for you

to seperate my thoughts

from the garden.

A Lullaby To Falling Asleep Alone

It is enough to murmur to

the night

and fall asleep in this lovely grass.

Shh!

Quitely, it is enough.

Sweet Simple Humanity

So often it is a casualty

to forget the oneness of life.

The wind that palpitates against

my skin

is the same wind playing wild

cards in your hair.

The bright sky, the staggered trees,

and the great temperature

of age burning a fever so sweltering

in our bones.

We are one,

though we know it not at times.

Passion

Passion is a currency

the members of the body

build a nation of gods

and goddesses with.

The nation is an art

comprised of the heart

and soul.

And so powerful it is

that the cavity of living

becomes full.

Powerful.

A universe.

This that passion truly is.

Threading A Thought

The words you create

are petty spoils you drop

with reasoned conviction.

These beliefs of personal

spell action aloud,

so that change may

be defined by

one who leads a

multitude.

I'm Me Inside

I wish someone would tell me why

we shed the skin we're born with

to take on the garments that other

people wear. No matter how

ill-fitting they are, we seem to

go to the ends of the earth—to die,

if it comes to that—to mend and

stitch and re-clothe ourselves over

and over. For why? Which purpose?

What is the idea?

We live an entire life

attaining the imperfections of others

because we don't like ours.

Constantly grabbing, snatching, and

yapping like hungry prey

wanting to be someone else, live

in someone else; we just simply

want the skin we weren't born

with because somehow that's the

only way to be accepted.

O' only, at least at some point

in life, we have to wake up

and smell the air that goes into *our*

lungs, not others.

Stretch our bones like they

actually speak and crack

with happiness to be a part of us.

If only examination would prompt it,

yell it even; the eyes that enjoy

the sun are our eyes with which

we can cry, laugh, and see through all

on our own. They are

no one else's.

The spirit, the soul, the

inner being has to change

and finally realize with triumph

that "I'm me inside."

The wheels have to rewind eventually,

like an old cassette tape—even

if slowly. Even if it's rusty,

awakening, shifting, and

Shaping, we must learn with gratitude

that we are born only as we are

to be who we are.

Flying

Time will fly

if we hasten it.

And if talking

to you all night

is a means

of growing wings,

I'll take it.

Because, who wouldn't

want to soar

with you?

Sitting Upon Purpose

I am proud to have the pride that mine eyes may see

who out there may lack uplift,

sunshines gift of positivity.

Worthy I am not,

to delude what is proof in pain.

But only in asking,

might I comfort thou's hurt with gain?

Growing,

I know you tiresomely prick,

though you sick of doing so.

Sometimes a beautiful being is

 flaw within wars fought

in the soul.

Perennial Predecessor

'Tis a wondrous thing in life

to think of all that we can kill,

in the forms and beings

survived by predecessors.

Yet we cannot pull the stars

down from the sky

and kill them, too.

For stars are for dreaming

and *dreams never die.*

Again and Again

Learn before you fall,

                fall before you learn,

and learn before you learn

                that you'll fall

after you've fallen.

Breath

The potions of nature

I drink of thee,

as if thou were

some caress of mortality.

Sweet river that rise,

there is no choke to your waves.

An ethereal poetry;

you whose many lives will save.

Those palms of reason

that open within a momentary rosebud,

even the wild

that mine eyes so secretly

infatuate.

Cannot but admire

the dimples in the mud.

A Daughter's Love

It washes those dishes

'til all the rough patches appear.

It makes few meals delicious

at any time of the year.

It turns down the beds

'til time for sheet washing.

It picks the sweetest reds

from apple trees green and cautioning.

It boils dark coffee

to have conversation in afternoon.

For now and thoughtfully,

a daughter listens over steaming brew.

Troubles and woes,

She has made them her own.

It as follows,

wisdom of another has made the child grown.

Full Grown Girl

Dinner stewed to chilliness

upon the rickety table

while we gathered around in unison to

attempt a prayer.

After the remains on plates and

bowls find themselves in

our stomachs,

the questions ask, the stories tell,

and the inquires explain.

All is well, 'til

Mamma asks me what I'd like

to be when I'm grown.

A nurse, a waitress, a scientist;

I throw the options around like

a billionaire with zero time for

such things,

then ponder my leftover pork

and beans with intensity.

Eleven years have packed their bags and left,

just for me to realize that,

despite all my dreams,

I'd like to be me.

Only problem was,

I took too long to figure it out.

Hopscotch

A butterfly played hopscotch

upon my skin earlier.

Then he took flight.

Where he went, I'll never

know.

But the recreational habit

of the little thing

brought peace.

And to my lips, a smile

better then the

medicine of any kiss

that I've known.

Frolic of Lazy

The last thought before I drop to sleep?

I know it not myself.

Only I know

that trees hide in the shadows

and blank skies move;

move steadily.

Steady.

Steady are the waves

here in the suburbs of childish play,

where the city growls

and yet I find myself idle

and my hands slow.

My ears timid to hear

and my legs stretched only to stretch,

because I know that this frolic

of lazy only lasts in youth.

Hottest Season

    Around the neck of the skies
hang white humble clouds.
Golden in their swift nimble;
moves roundabout.
    The Afternoon courtesies with
exaggeration;
    the weather herself seems
keen and curious.

    Ever still, and slowly,
trees hug shallow breezes soft.
Where
    birds lounge in shady lofts.
    There are smiles like peace
after a stormy rage,
    and yet summer isn't summer
without your hand over mine
upon this scribbled page.

Welcome Home

The first thing I'd like to show you

upon first walking into my house

is the glee with which I set my

table.

My plates will be pretty, and my spoons

will glimmer as if happy to feed you.

Everything tidy, set, even so nicely

stable.

The napkins are arrayed a certain way,

upon first glance you look,

as if happy to see them folded over

apart.

Because darling, my home, my dinner,

my beheld adoration for you is spread

like a welcome home from the

heart.

The Garment

Dignity—

the highest bestowment

a man can die with

may also be the richest

thing he'll ever own.

Treasure chest of his heart,

where the key can only

be shaped in the form

of his tender moral.

A man can not ask

for a better garment

to wear;

for this fitteth him best.

How to be A Man

A heavy handed tool

is for burying your heavier pride,

covering it with dirt in humility,

giving it chance to air dry.

Love Letters

Love letters are sacred obituaries

in that, after their writer has counted breaths under

the stars no longer,

the handwritten nuances hold new meaning each sunrise

that they are read.

I am more than aware of how the clouds bicker

 with the storms.

But a love letter cannot feel the wind nor

 the rain in such an instance.

Because you are already right now within your mind's

eye, remembering one particular letter.

Its words remind you, in a million ways,

how such fruit tasted during your moments

of loneliness.

The page sits out to dry like linen by

the fire.

He never forgot you my dear.

Reminiscent Fate

You've forgotten all of the ways you remind me.

You remind me of

    wistful sundays

spent listening to the water run,

trying to hush itself.

It slips through and out

like the stretch of some ivory sweetness.

You remind me of

    traffic and brandy.

That west coast loneliness casts a spell

on us all, don't it?

But I remember you like vodka and cherry.

You remind me of

    city flora.

Night lights and kiss fights, all beating

around bushes of old museums and churches.

Because you know I'll go walking and exploring

anywhere with you, long as I feel the

sacred wrap of your arm around my shoulders.

You've forgotten all the ways

      you remind me.

But by now, I'm sure I've

forgotten all the ways that

time grew old.

It's a stale, bittersweet thing.

But in some regard,

a thing to think of you by.

What Comes Around

Sometimes my strength,

and yours—it is spent.

Gone like breath 'til the

air is given back to us.

The Hypocrite

You,

right there.

You

who plays innocent.

Slithering in blithering

hisses.

Hiding behind the veneer

of Judas kisses.

You will never be innocent

when you're as rotten as your insides.

You eat your smiling lies,

and when the plate becomes empty,

you play and dance like a friendly enemy.

Cremation

So often I've breathed a little prayer.

One offered to God,

that would ask him to take me back

whence the place he spewed me forth.

I've tried a dream

in wondering if my existence was thought

up in a place where the birds sang

and the primrose bloomed.

The outcome is incomprehensible.

My dearest Lord, you've made a mistake.

I am the thorn amidst all this beauty.

Even the sparrow cannot but pluck

bitter worms from my footprints.

my name spoils like a cask,

an unkempt slur of sour drought.

He who brought about such a thing

must slaughter it, take it back,

make it disappear into nothing.

For the sake of the woods,

the planet is a child—all grown and built

of wisdom founded in simple dirt.

O' even simple dirt hath more intelligence

than I!

It knows the seasons, the nutrients,

the growth, the decay—

who am I to say

that I ought to be buried in it

when I die?

A precious mistake that is!

wistful

The clouds move like the

volume of a thousand seas.

Pressure hereby as the wind

storms past in a flitting breeze.

Trains rolling a little off,

wishing me farewell as they go.

For I do indeed find it eerie;

the passings, the journeys, the go-tos,

the disguised answers and good wills.

All of it. I am so wistful for change.

But only if...

If only I'd stay young

as the seasons fly; a wish—

a gift it'd be—to be wise

without being old.

O' alas, I'm so wistful!

Rebuke

Your passions are fleeting

in diabolical spaces of time.

You, young woman,

hath not completed a thing

unless you've put aside your

pillow filled with fanciful dreams

and actually dug the dirt

to find the flower.

Justice in Question

The one virtue

of one nation.

By leave, where has it taken itself?

It seems,

for certain,

no more does it attempt to exist.

It's fled us

because we do not

uphold it as everyone else.

Crowded societies,

and yet silence is new.

The hell upon which we insist.

To Critics

Empty praises, foolish game,

I **care not** for you.

Blared critic on channeled news,

I **despise** you.

Diversity so popular nowadays,

I ask only that you

friend me.

For they that gaze behind mirth,

I spit them behind me

as well.

Finding God

(When God Finds You)

Often, it's a wonder

to imagine what the clouds must think

when they travel the world

to see the calluses of our wars,

outlined in the chins of our countries;

lifted up and tilted downward

in matter of fact motions,

only to say that nothing is inadvertently abstract

unless one speaks of motive.

That cloud yonder,

he frowns with his soul bleeding clear,

occasionally drying his face in the grass

and giving way for prayer with the sun.

If with heaviness, mortality did not at times

look to the elements in the so distant heavens,

it is believable that we would wax death—

a romantic favorability against spiritual struggle,

particularly the struggle that leads to life!

If I Could Do Something With My Hair

If I could do something with my hair today,

I would take it down,

untangle the knots of spray,

and comb it into a pile of leaves

that sit atop a tree——lazily.

I'd live for none other a purpose

than to make conversation with the wind.

Because, this illusion of beauty...

It puts me to sleep.

And I believe

a woman can be a direction;

no woman should be sleep-walking

 in life.

A Wife knows better——a Mother, too

——and a Sister can love her brother

more easily than anyone else.

If I could do something with my hair today,

I'd pin all my leaves and show you

your soul,

because it's there.

Maybe it's the wind.

Maybe it's condensation

from all the weeping of a hard time.

But there are more important things

to this fatality of being

than some veneer that one can peel.

I'm not sure what sort of story

we are writing,

but we are breath, we are words,

we are laughter.

We are tears, we are

anger, and we are blood.

Divinity is a scalpel to which the anatomy

of this story ends and begins

constantly.

If I could do something with my hair today,

I'd plant it

so that another tree would grow.

The branches would be long and high;

that another in search of

his or her soul

would at least have a place

to sit.

Religion That I Am

Religion that I am,

I let slumber

slip off my shoulder

gracefully in a heap

onto the grass.

I

become all things

in the surgery of the AM.

Sun rises

between my ribs

and takes an elevator

down between my nexus.

My morning, my!

Her plum biscotti skies

open my heart

to ways of existing

like I never have before.

Should it smite me,

easily I wouldn't know.

But how

I must live

(I *want* to live).

Should the dementia

of this cursed life

let me not,

then rebel I will,

religion that I am.

The Gift

When life gives you a lie,

wrap it up

and hand it back.

Because when you allow truth

to be the assembly of

decision,

the greatest gift of all

is freedom.

Error In Light

The only way to

take pride in a mistake

is to learn from it.

Quirks

Enter here,

through that corridor.

Then go outside and look around.

Underneath

 the blush of the night,

you may notice my little town.

Call her;

she'll come soon,

wearing eccentric seasons like a gown.

Housekeeper

a century aged,

she is a neighborhood bereft of sound.

Innkeeper,

doorway guard.

She laughs when she is weak.

Through here,

down a few roads.

No, I do not know all of these streets.

But go,

her house is a castle

built under the memories she keeps.

Opened hall,

raised high on stitches.

For belonging is a pillow of many sleeps.

In here,

is a room of hesitation.

Folding and unfolding of particular hands.

She knows

all that notice.

They are familiar to these pebbled lands.

Walking forth.

These quirks, they're for

proving individuality in woman and man.

No surprise

that this little town

is a lover of kinds,

and she loves peculiarity when it stands.

The Repose Of A Dim Sighted Night

The evening is warm

inside this home I've made for myself.

The mist settled between the evergreens,

the outside looking in

as I take my hair down to a

Hozier song.

Some of the swell in one of the

violins sends me moving into tingles

across the room.

Apart of me (not a part of me).

Suddenly my thirst is quenched.

The silhouette of words being sung

like a backdrop against my movements.

A bird buries its burden silently in the night

as it flies over my shingles.

I tend to feel its breeze fluttering

against the curtains of my soul.

Peace is goodness; a slow dance

with one's thoughts.

Lost in books and outstretched toes,

the evening is warm,

but yearning is the gift for

finally a little sleep.

Cancer

If all there was of you

was your tailbone and your crumbs,

still happy I'd be

to care for you,

even if it were your unspoken words

and idle thumbs.

If all there was of you

was your silver kinks and your age,

still happy I'd be

to care for you,

even if it were your incomprehensible

affliction and sickly rage.

If all there was of you

was your dense grasp and your jawbone,

Still happy I'd be

to care for you,

even if it were your tares; the terrors

of being alone.

Though the crux of this cross

may be cancer,

I cross my heart

to let love be the answer.

But if all there was of you

was nothing,

my beloved, dear sweet friend,

"nothing" was not the end

I was dreaming of.

Nevertheless,

if all there was of you

was your dignity and your sweet smile,

still happy I'd be

to care for you.

Even if it were just your memory

On The Edge of a Dream - Atalie Rachael

stuck in every crack

of every mile

for as long as I live.

Lovely Thing

I'll call you beautiful everyday,

but on the days you're most down

I'm going to call you lovely.

I'm going to remind you in all the ways I can

how much you mean to me.

All the times you've embroidered my

life with grace and lesson;

they serve as reminders of what I'm

reminding you—that you are more than

beautiful, more than bright, more

than what the darkness has made you

to be, and more than what the universe

conspires your existence and circumstance

to be.

You are more than everything.

You are a lovely thing.

Advice

Diamonds can be lost in an orchard

millions of times, but a heart can only be found once.

Wherever a heart is found, abide by the lungs it gives you,

because whatever

passes through must be taken care of with

absolute frailty.

Curfew

No great poet has to tell you

whether you are loving

or leaving.

It is always good to give

your heart a curfew,

for too far have

the stupidest of things gone

when they were not lent a

simple night of rest.

Domestic Affairs and The Feminist

Hands loaded with bread flour.

Tablespoons measuring potato powder.

The mind behind these actions

asks if that's all there is for rations.

Rationally exquisite, the way her hair is up;

the way she takes on jobs minorly tough.

She is the peace in peacemaking.

Doing all the oddities, the dishes, the knee-scraping

and making up for what others forgot in provision.

The rules are new——she's the revision.

Freedom is a price unpaid, waiting awake

only to find nothing changes.

But there sure is bread to make.

Dinner makes the table pretty, and her tired

but sacrificing dreams are the universe's desire.

And maybe that's the whole point of it all:

To work and earn thankfulness, a different

equality unequal.

Even then, that is the beauty of difference.

She struggles to learn lessons; her biggest hindrance.

To see that patience is like a weaving tool

and hope is the silver thread designated cruel.

Striving accomplishment, satisfaction, and rest.

She knows she's a different kind of feminist.

The Insecure Writer and The Resurrection

How often I've wanted to sit by a grave

and pluck the stems from its side.

The hues of flowers

against a cast clove colored

tombstone;

they literally mock the idea of death.

And how often I've dreamed of doing more

than sitting nearest an earth packed plot.

For instance, to dig it up,

throw aside the sod in showers

—and look,

there they are. The bones of the body.

The parts of the poet; the mentor, the friend.

I've awakened him, and now see his confusion

in how he gazes at the pieces

of what he once was.

Hastily, I must put him together.

Socket by socket. Vessel by vessel. Cell by cell.

He rises, looking at the others around him,
wondering what became of mankind—if indeed man was kind.

He looks at me, one eyebrow raised
"What is all this, and who are you?"

I take my writing journal from my pack.
Opening it, I spread the pages out like a delicate fleece
and I say,
"I brought us lunch."

Right then and there, he smiles knowingly.
We are going to have a feast.

Unsettled Wisdom

Clean the shelves.

Move the rooms.

I rearrange in different spots

to fit the patterns

taking place in my thoughts.

All of it feels

like I'm racing the god

that I made up inside,

when all I do

is move with the crowd;

finding the next

Been there done that.

Satisfaction,

I move with them.

Taking in their apparel;

the sights of all as one.

And next day

I'm picking strawberries,

with a song part way

upon my lips.

For I believed within

that I've found everything.

I haven't.

Many and many have,

but when we sit to muse,

we bring a thing glorious

in its flesh;

'til it becomes thin,

starved, and without.

Without—in many ways

—crying the tears

of our own pride.

We'd confess we are lonely,

but it's so much more

found deep down

inside the chronicles

of our hearts;

Through decades.

I'm not sure what it is,

but all I can say

is that I care too much

about all of these things

to ever do much.

And only that

helps me understand

a little thing about time.

Because indeed,

time is medicine

and medicine is time.

The former, a healer.

The latter? An even better healer.

Moving forward,

all I can do is move the rooms

and clean the shelves

just once more.

Keepsake

Forget and forgive,

for in forgiving

you are giving

life all anew.

Familiar Face

Soft edges within a thorn drenched of its sweet nectar.

Barren to the naked core,

like weakness before it hatches.

I almost can feel my heritage adrift.

Pattering echoes settled into mindful oblivion

while walking.

Strange lilac gray (branched away);

stripped dead to be torn alive.

Yet, like an unburied seed, there is you.

A wholesome find, I found light

deliberate with intent.

Outstretched embrace spelling home,

cozied up in the back of the woods.

Upon my furrowed face, I am solely touched.

It's good to see you again.

Let The Bad Time Pass

Your reflection,

how it confuses you,

friend.

The way your gaze

melts into rain

all upon your tile floor,

like a last breath after

war.

But rest assured,

your sobs will soon smile

and your relief will shine.

It's just your diamond,

it got covered with a little

mud in the

typhoon.

Motherhood And Its Moment

Almost all mothers can hear their daughters

tip-toed slippered feet down the hallway.

Because as they tiptoe, they stop

a little, and go a little,

hanging thoughts on the walls like stockings

as they pause.

Whatever little daughters do, they leave hints

like needles in haystacks into their world

and mothers must learn what that darned

but beautiful child is actually all about,

for this bares a resemblance

to true love.

Pea Pods

I saw a man dig into his porch today,

his day old beard shining like cacti in the sun.

He seemed to be searching for something

under all the bridges he built in life.

I wanted to ask him his name,

but couldn't gather much about him

(except that he was my father).

A man passionate about justice amongst

many other thorns growing along his highways

that I at times forget I once was a

pea pod sitting in his lap,

snuggling myself to sleep amongst his wisdom.

Many people hate that, but who am I

to care?

It's good to be jealous of something good.

But now that I'm here today

planting things nearest our porch,

I sense that I am under yet another bridge

of his,

looking up at the architecture;

feeling a new thing peeking its way out of

my being.

That is love. I feel as if I know how

to love a man

because I loved him.

I grew arms for someone to crawl

home to.

And to look up at this bridge

and all its spokes kissing the sky,

it's hard to believe in a little thing

like womanhood.

I'm not ideal;

then again, my father never raised me to be.

It takes guts to build and grow

and make a porch for a home.

And he did so much more than that.

He raised a daughter,

and she planted beautiful things

like peapods.

Pride

Her vulnerability was a murmur

running through the backstreets.

Softly, her tiptoed steps accompanied

the city's musings like a thousand beats.

Out To Dry

A thought.

I don't know how to put it,

but I'd put it out to dry

in the sun.

How often it is

that I demand too much from life,

when life should be the one

demanding from me.

Demanding that I make a difference

and let my shoes be the

stepping stones.

Let it be known

it were mine

that added to a mortal garden,

and that all my spruce

made decorative use

of imagination.

How else

would you therefore prove

that selfish incentive grows nullity?

And that which has been mentioned,

its intention can be no more than

piled rot—a lot of useless wither.

Nay, I've settled me;

put it out to the sun.

There it will dry,

and the nutrient of contentment

will leave it there.

Fortitude

Wherever I go,

I keep you in my soul.

Like a dandelion without wither,

this precious intent

comes forth and hither

to remind me

I am not entirely whole

unless I've decided

to stop being alone.

Mistakes

I studied my mistakes today

and—as if another soul

wasn't around

—they spoke to me.

With a hand gently resting

and a voice spoken softly,

I heard:

"Thy work is far from over.

Start over before you

grow older."

And with that, the hand

melted from my shoulder,

but the voice stayed.

No matter the frustration or hurt,

my mistakes told me to

never be afraid.

Aphorism

I feel as if there are

shades to the

sunshine we create

in this life.

And all it takes is

a subsequent blending

of the rules.

Appetite

A godless appetite will never savor piety,

because the flavor of purity

is that which death tastes

with such sneer.

Suffer Not This Distress

It's compressed.

The time fleeting,

beating

within my breast.

The minutes.

A precise but infinite

score,

traced by the roots

of unowned experience.

It's twofold.

The hours seethe,

teethe

straight into the cold.

On The Edge of a Dream - Atalie Rachael

Nothing distracts

like politics chasing

scruples of split lands and

apocalyptic ends.

Temple

It is wrong to be asked

to be worshipped,

for it is vanity.

But it is within deserving

to be

r e s p e c t e d.

Mythical Cure

If the rain cannot

cure itself of falling,

then why should you

cure the passionate little

stream that flows

just below the bridge

of your soul?

Servant's Neglect

Give a dying man a cocktail

on a sponge

and bring it to his lips.

If it drips into his cheekbone

rather than his mouth,

then something has cried

for him other than

he for himself.

This is the way the world works.

One has love before

the last sigh, or they don't.

Sometimes there's just simplicity

without relational meaning,

and that is easily one of the most

heartbreaking ways to leave this life.

Don't Worry, My Lovely

Don't worry, my lovely.

You are most positively

a beautiful thing.

Relatively charming—

a most neat package

I'd open always.

To prove my love devout;

this, characteristically,

I could do to befriend

thee.

Don't worry, my lovely,

the world and its ugly

hath no love for you.

But I do.

Compassionately,

I'd ask you

To stay lovely,

but to never worry.

Prophesying Humility

You learn by trembling at your

own master.

Giving into hardship in trial

by error.

Standing in time, it is with

eventuality

that your own hard-working hands

will become

glamorous by your own eyes.

In reality,

you will understand all is not

for granted.

And you will master the better

of things to come.

Like mountain rain, wisdom will

garnish you.

It will ask of lastly that you

be quiet

after your work has been done.

For The Sole Reason Of It

Intimacy is a softly swinging foot;

the toes polished decently,

the heel bare.

Barely soft,

but a little calloused.

A little too step driven.

The one who watches that foot

may notice its need for a sandal.

Wouldn't we all protect

a loved one's sole

when he or she tenderly bruises

and needs the affection of loyalty?

Make Me Bloom

Understanding.

The greatest soil

you could put atop me,

and I would bloom

sweet rain

in your sky full

of lilac.

Going Places

The open road before me,

it creases along the folds of time.

Generous, it wills me farther

with the speed-bumps assigned.

It whispers me lessons

while chasing the sunset against the grain.

We share smiles amidst sad,

and sometimes we are our only fame.

Dancing on roofs of grassy concrete,

somehow I am sped by the season's change.

This in my bosoms close.

It cannot be denied that this journey is strange,

as if it were another in my ride.

Jealousy—not one of my greatest graces.

The road though, please do come along.

For I know not of you, but I'm going places.

Learning To Discern

All is an asset,

and all assets are blessings.

By which you may ask,

what wonder could that possibly mean?

If one can hope,

that is a learned aspiration

for things to come.

If one can love,

that is a divine attribute

provided for us all.

If one can relinquish,

that is proper in

its sense of letting go.

If one can ache,

hate, and question,

it is human nature

brought out to the fullest.

It is these aspects of

human nature

that we must learn

to either rekindle

or burn alive,

in as much

as we would burn

any evil unbecoming

of its own motive.

The Puzzle

Home finds its way

back to everyone

eventually.

Whether it's now,

tomorrow,

or years afar;

it comes in fragments.

When you

find the pieces,

you must slowly

make the puzzle.

Connect the pictures,

the elements,

and the new streets.

You'll slowly see

where it is exactly

that you belong.

Roman Goddess Of Dawn

5 AM—

A chorus of birds.

I have naught to do

But to crawl out of bed

and join them.

They bring the rising sun

with them;

though I've been told,

supposedly, it's a cruel thing

to make a god of a thing.

My God,

this morning the horizon

has strawberries in its hands,

and everything about awakening

smells like honeydew.

So, I think I'll stay awake, too.

On The Edge of a Dream - Atalie Rachael

Poetic Epilogue

I have my own words

written before me

as a testament

that I lived on the breath

and breadth of life,

so that I can at least say

I was a human being

before I died

and became whatever

God willed for me to

become.

Acknowledgments

— ✿ ❀ —

The ultimate risk is to live. Sometimes in living there are dreams to fulfill. My dream indefinitely was the writing and publishing of this book, and I would never have been able to do it without these people to thank.

Firstly, thank you to my parents. To my dad, who only vaguely knew that I was writing this book and remained a foundational inspiration for all things within my life. He's taught me everything, and blesses my life constantly with rebukes, wisecracks, and advice. He is home to me.

To my mom, who also only vaguely knew of this book, and offered unconditional support through her acceptance of my poetry. Her love and hugs are everything. She also would most likely attest to the fact that I don't act enough like a lady. And so I hope this book makes up the classier side of me and honors her wish that I am less of a tomboy in the process.

Thank you to my best friend, Alyssa. She's been a part of this book every step of the way, and will never understand the gratitude and love I have for her. Her encouragement, ideas, thoughts, and edits have made this book what it is. And can we have a moment for the book cover itself? She designed that (from scratch)!

Thank you to Jenny, Grace, Fil, and Emily. Your love, support, and friendship has meant a lot.

Thank you to the poetry forums and literary journals that have published my work in the past (i.e *Leaves Of Ink, The Voices Project, AllPoetry*, etc.).

Thank you to IngramSpark for the opportunity to self publish and be in control of every single decision along the way.

Last but not least... Thank you dear reader, for believing in me enough to buy this book, and for keeping some essence of not only a dream, but poetry alive.

Thank you!

About The Author

— ✿ ❀ —

Born and raised in the Metro Detroit area, poetess Atalie Rachael hopes to inspire others and be a fluent provision for creativity. Her interests almost always lie in saying something unusual to encompass life's beauty, pain, and bittersweet touches.